The Life Cycle of a

SUNFLOWER

Philip Parker

Illustrated by

Jackie Harland

Reading Consultant:

Diana Bentley

The Bookwright Press
New York · 1988

Life Cycles

The Life Cycle of an Ant
The Life Cycle of a Butterfly
The Life Cycle of a Frog
The Life Cycle of a Rabbit
The Life Cycle of a Stickleback
The Life Cycle of a Sunflower

First published in the
United States in 1988 by
The Bookwright Press
387 Park Avenue South
New York, NY 10016

First published in 1988 by
Wayland (Publishers) Limited
61 Western Road, Hove
East Sussex, BN3 1JD, England

© Copyright 1988 Wayland (Publishers) Limited

Library of Congress Cataloging-in-Publication Data
Parker, Philip
    The life cycle of a sunflower/Philip Parker.
        p.   cm.
    Bibliography: p.
    Includes index.
    Summary: Describes the life cycle of a sunflower, from
the naming of its parts to a discussion of reproduction and
pollinization. Includes simple projects and questions.
    ISBN 0-531-18191-X
    1. Sunflowers—Life cycle—Juvenile literature. 2. Plant
life cycles—Juvenile literature. (1. Sunflowers—Life
cycle. 2. Plant life cycles.) I. Title.   87–32632
QK495.C74P37 1988   CIP
583′.55—dc 19   AC

Typeset in the UK by DP Press Limited, Sevenoaks, Kent
Printed by Casterman S.A., Belgium

Notes for parents and teachers
Each title in this series has been specially written and
designed as a first natural history book for young readers.
For less able readers there are introductory captions,
while the more detailed text explains each illustration.

Contents

All the words that are
in **bold** are explained in
the glossary on page 31.

Sunflowers in the summer.

Look at these gigantic flowers. They have bright yellow petals that make them look like the sun. We call them sunflowers. Sunflowers have very tall **stalks** and they grow higher than you! To stay in the ground sunflowers have long **roots**.

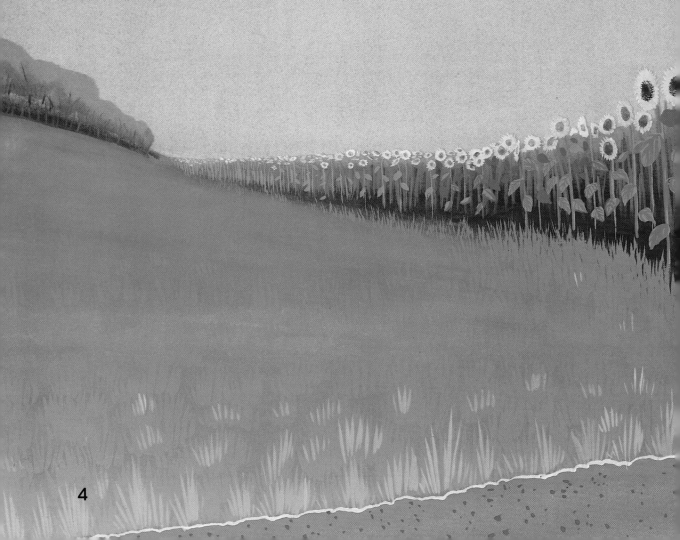

6

The sunflower makes a powder called **pollen**.

This flower head is as big as a dinner plate. In the middle of the flower head are the parts that make new sunflowers. Some of these parts make pollen. Other parts will hold new sunflower **seeds**.

A bee visits the sunflower and takes some pollen.

Do you know why sunflowers have bright yellow petals? It is to attract bees. When a bee lands on the flower head it eats the sweet-tasting pollen. As the bee crawls over the flower some of the pollen sticks to its legs and body.

9

The bee carries the pollen to another sunflower.

The bee leaves the flower head and flies to another sunflower. The bee still has a lot of pollen on its legs and body. As it crawls over the new flower, the pollen brushes off onto the parts that will hold the new seeds. This is called **pollination**.

The new seeds.

Many grains of pollen stick to the flower head. The pollen is so tiny that you can hardly see it. The pollen and the parts of the flower that hold the new seeds join together. This is called **fertilization**. Now the new seeds will begin to form.

13

The seeds in the autumn.

When autumn comes the parent plant is old, and its petals are brown and crinkled. This plant will soon die, but the new seeds are almost ready to fall. Look at the pattern of the seeds in the flower head.

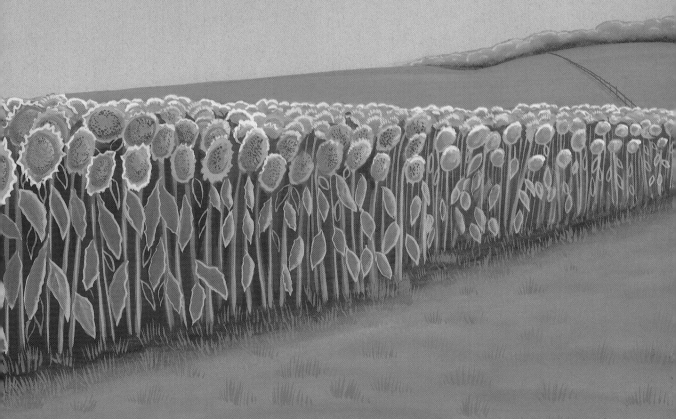

A bird takes a seed.

A bird flies to the old sunflower and clings to the flower head. It is looking for seeds to eat. It uses its beak to peck out new seeds. As it flies away it drops a seed on the ground.

The seed in the winter.

The seed lies on the ground and the wind covers it with soil and fallen leaves. Winter arrives and the seed stays under the cold ground, but when the winter has passed, the spring sun heats up the ground. This warms up the cold seed.

The seed grows a root in the spring.

Then, the spring rains fall on the ground. The seed takes in the water and starts to get bigger. A root begins to grow out of the seed and down into the ground. This root will hold the plant in the ground and take in more water to help it grow.

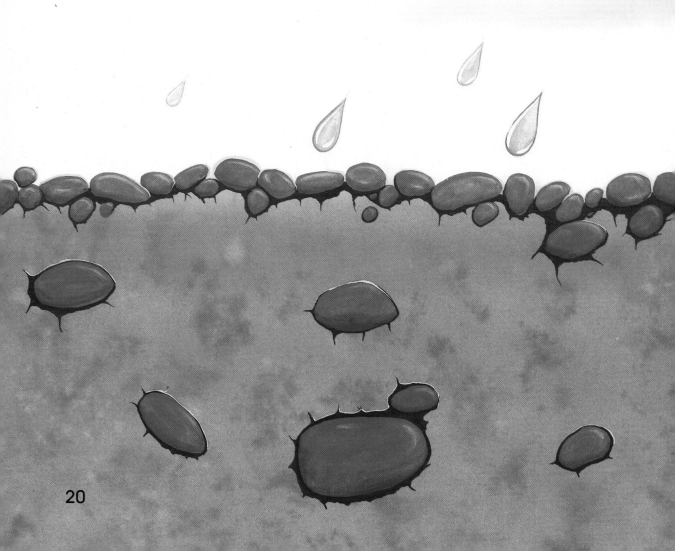

21

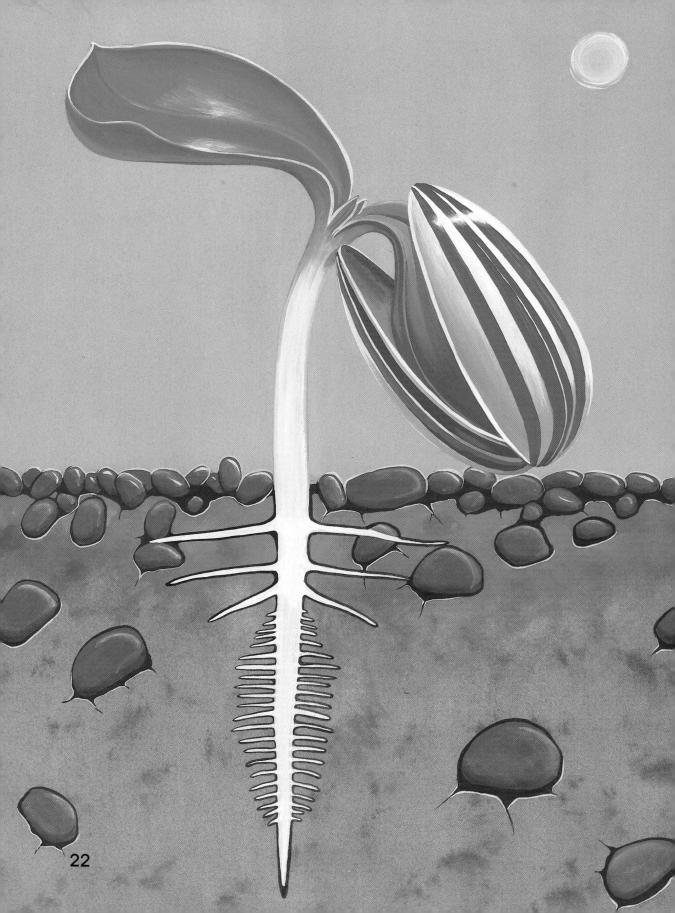

Look at the tiny stalk and leaves.

The seed grows a young stalk. We call this a **shoot**. The shoot grows upward, pushing the green inner parts of the seed up into the air. These green parts are called **seed leaves**. When the seed leaves are pushed above the ground they open out.

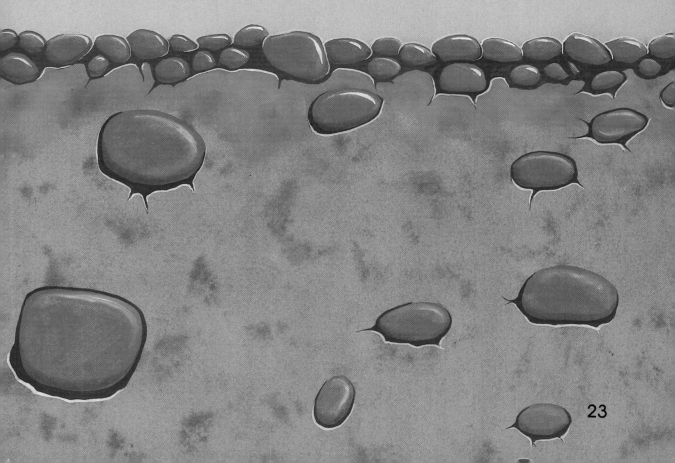

The young sunflower grows more leaves.

At first the sunflower uses food stored in the seed leaves to help it grow. After a few days different leaves begin to grow. These leaves use sunlight to help them make food. The sunflower now grows very quickly.

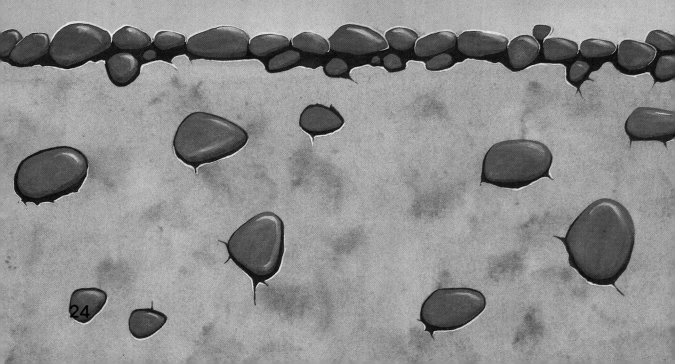

25

The big flowers open in the summer.

At the beginning of the summer a large, green **bud** grows on top of the stalk. Inside it is the new flower. Soon it will open and the new flower will begin to make pollen. Can you remember what happens next?

Growing a sunflower.

If you would like to grow a sunflower, you will need some sunflower seeds, some soil, a seed tray and a big pot. It is important to plant sunflower seeds in the spring so that the flowers can come out in the summer. Fill the seed tray with soil. Make a hole with your finger and put a seed into it. Cover the seed with soil. Put five or six seeds in the soil in this way and water them. Now they will begin to grow.

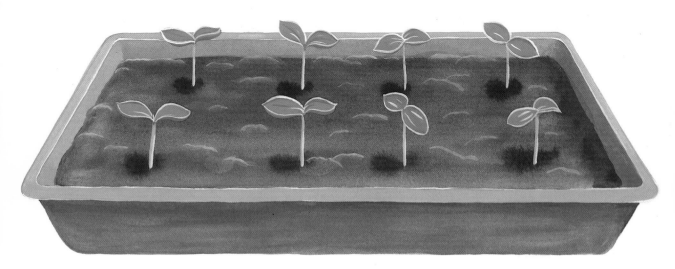

When four or five leaves have grown, fill the big pot with soil. Make a hole with your finger. Put the roots of the best sunflower into the hole and cover them with soil. Pour a little water on the soil from time to time and watch your sunflower grow. Put the pot outside in the garden. What creatures will come to visit your sunflower?

The life cycle of a sunflower.

How many stages of the life cycle of a sunflower can you remember?

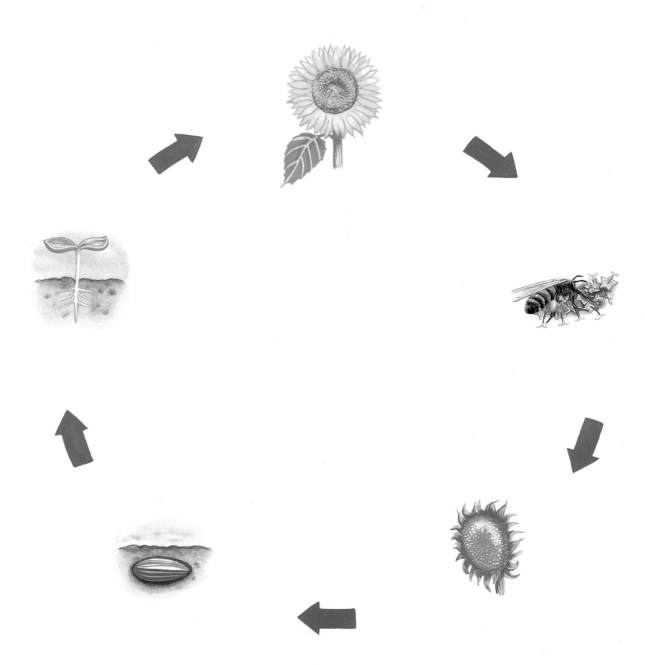

Glossary

Bud A flower before it opens.

Fertilization Putting pollen on the parts of the flower that will hold the new seeds. After fertilization the new seeds can begin to form.

Pollen A fine powder made by most flowers. Pollen is needed to make new seeds.

Pollination Placing pollen from one flower onto another to make a seed start to form.

Roots The part of a plant that grows down into the ground and takes in water to help the plant grow.

Seed leaves The first leaves that come out of a seed. They give the young plant food.

Seeds The parts of a flower that will grow into new plants.

Shoot The shoot is the first part of a plant to grow out of the ground.

Stalks Stems. The parts of plants that make them stand up. The flower grows at the end of the stalk.

Finding out more

Here are some books to read to find out
more about sunflowers and other plants.

Amazing World of Plants by Elizabeth Marcus (Troll Associat
   1984)
Discovering Flowering Plants by Jennifer Coldrey (Bookwrig
   Press, 1987)
The Flower Book by Anne Orange (Lerner Publications, 197
How Plants Grow by Steve Parker (Franklin Watts, 1985)
Look at Flowers by Rena K. Kirkpatrick (Raintree Publishers,
   1985)

Index